# DO THE WO GENDER EQUALITY

## COMMITTING TO THE UN'S SUSTAINABLE DEVELOPMENT GOALS

JULIE KNUTSON

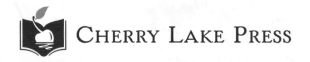

Published in the United States of America by Cherry Lake Publishing Group
Ann Arbor, Michigan
www.cherrylakepublishing.com

Reading Adviser: Beth Walker Gambro, MS, Ed., Reading Consultant, Yorkville, IL
Photo Credits: © Odua Images/Shutterstock.com, cover, 1; © Riccardo Mayer/Shutterstock.com, 5;
Infographic From The Sustainable Development Goals Report 2020, by United Nations Department of Economic
and Social Affairs © 2020 United Nations. Reprinted with the permission of the United Nations, 7; © Monkey
Business Images/Shutterstock.com, 9; © RomanR/Shutterstock.com, 10; © Giannis Papanikos/Shutterstock.
com, 13; © Anton Ivanov/Shutterstock.com, 14; © Mikolaj Barbanell/Shutterstock.com, 16; © Prabhjt S.
Kalsi/Shutterstock.com, 19; © Krakenimages.com/Shutterstock.com, 20; © Andrey Yershov/Shutterstock.
com, 23; © Naresh777/Shutterstock.com, 24; © Ms Jane Campbell/Shutterstock.com, 27

Cherry Lake Press is an imprint of Cherry Lake Publishing Group.

Library of Congress Cataloging-in-Publication Data
Names: Knutson, Julie, author.
Title: Do the work! : gender equality / Julie Knutson.
Description: Ann Arbor, Michigan : Cherry Lake Publishing, 2022. | Series: Committing to the UN's sustainable
    development goals | Audience: Grades 4-6
Identifiers: LCCN 2021036388 (print) | LCCN 2021036389 (ebook) | ISBN 9781534199279 (hardcover) |
    ISBN 9781668900413 (paperback) | ISBN 9781668906170 (ebook) | ISBN 9781668901854 (pdf)
Subjects: LCSH: Gender identity—Juvenile literature. | Sex discrimination against women—Juvenile literature. |
    Equality—Juvenile literature.
Classification: LCC HQ18.552 K68 2022 (print) | LCC HQ18.552 (ebook) | DDC 305.3—dc23
LC record available at https://lccn.loc.gov/2021036388
LC ebook record available at https://lccn.loc.gov/2021036389

Cherry Lake Publishing Group would like to acknowledge the work of the Partnership for 21st Century
Learning, a Network of Battelle for Kids. Please visit http://www.battelleforkids.org/networks/p21
for more information.

Printed in the United States of America
Corporate Graphics

The content of this publication has not been approved by the United Nations and does not reflect the views of the
United Nations or its officials or Member States. For more information on the Sustainable Development Goals please visit
https://www.un.org/sustainabledevelopment.

# ABOUT THE AUTHOR

Julie Knutson is an author-educator who writes extensively about global citizenship and the
Sustainable Development Goals. Her previous book, *Global Citizenship: Engage in the Politics
of a Changing World* (Nomad Press, 2020), introduces key concepts about 21st-century
interconnectedness to middle grade and high school readers. She hopes that this series will
inspire young readers to take action and embrace their roles as changemakers in the world.

# TABLE OF CONTENTS

CHAPTER 1
**Meet the SDGs** ........................................................ 4

CHAPTER 2
**Why Do We Have Goals?** ..................................... 12

CHAPTER 3
**Do the Work! Contribute to the Goals at Home .....** 18

CHAPTER 4
**Do the Work! Contribute to the Goals at School ...** 22

CHAPTER 5
**Do the Work! Contribute to the Goals
in Your Community** .............................................. 26

EXTEND YOUR LEARNING ................................................. 29

FURTHER RESEARCH ..................................................... 30

GLOSSARY ............................................................... 31

INDEX .................................................................. 32

# CHAPTER 1

# Meet the SDGs

In Malawi, Chief Theresa Kachindamoto works to end child marriages. In Mexico, journalist Lydia Cacho Ribeiro exposes **human trafficking** networks that exploit women and girls. In India, 70,000 young people march on the International Day of the Girl to demand the right to attend school. And across the world, more than 300,000 "Girls Who Code" show that girls can program a computer every bit as well as their male peers.

Every day across the globe, courageous **advocates** stand up, speak out, and take action. Their goal? To build a **gender**-equal world. This means making education available to all. It means eliminating all forms of violence against women and girls. It means the promise of equal pay for equal work. It means creating a world where all children, regardless of gender, have the same opportunities.

Water collection often falls on the shoulders of women and girls.

These include the chance to run businesses or lead governments, choose their own spouse, and decide if and when they want to have a family. It means a world in which people can freely express their **gender identities** without fear of harm.

Along with millions of others, these advocates work toward the **United Nations**' (UN) fifth **Sustainable** Development Goal (SDG), "Gender Equality." They want the goal to become a reality for each person on the planet by 2030.

# What Are the SDGs?

There are 17 SDGs, ranging from "No Poverty" (SDG 1) to "Partnership for the Goals" (SDG 17). In between, you'll find "Quality Education" (SDG 4), "Decent Work and Economic Growth" (SDG 8), and "Climate Action" (SDG 13). The point of the SDGs, announced by the UN in 2015, is to create a road map for a more just and sustainable world. The timeline for making significant progress on these goals is 15 years.

"Gender Equality" is the fifth goal on the list. While much progress has been to advance women's rights over the past 100 years, *much more* remains to be done. Around the world, 155 countries still have at least one law limiting women's economic potential. In addition, 41 countries ban women from working in certain factory jobs. In 29 countries, women cannot work at night. In Russia, women are barred from holding 456 jobs. In the United States, the average woman would have to work an extra *42* days per year to earn the same amount as the average man. That difference is even greater for people of color.

[ 21ST CENTURY SKILLS LIBRARY ]

# 5 GENDER EQUALITY

# ACHIEVE GENDER EQUALITY AND EMPOWER ALL WOMEN AND GIRLS

## DESPITE IMPROVEMENTS, FULL GENDER EQUALITY REMAINS UNREACHED

FEWER GIRLS ARE FORCED INTO EARLY MARRIAGE

• • •

MORE WOMEN ARE IN LEADERSHIP ROLES

### WOMEN MUST BE REPRESENTED FAIRLY

IN PANDEMIC-RELATED LEADERSHIP ROLES

### WOMEN REPRESENT

**25%**
IN NATIONAL PARLIAMENTS
(2020)

**36%**
IN LOCAL GOVERNMENT
(2020)

## LOCKDOWNS ARE INCREASING THE RISK OF VIOLENCE AGAINST WOMEN AND GIRLS

PHYSICAL ———— SEXUAL ———— PSYCHOLOGICAL

CASES OF DOMESTIC VIOLENCE **HAVE INCREASED BY 30%** IN SOME COUNTRIES

### WOMEN ARE ON THE FRONT LINES OF FIGHTING THE CORONAVIRUS

### WOMEN ACCOUNT FOR 70% OF HEALTH AND SOCIAL WORKERS

**WOMEN BEAR ADDITIONAL HOUSEHOLD BURDENS DURING THE PANDEMIC**

↓ ↓ ↓

WOMEN ALREADY SPEND ABOUT THREE TIMES AS MANY HOURS IN UNPAID DOMESTIC AND CARE WORK AS MEN

SUSTAINABLE DEVELOPMENT G**O**ALS

# What Is Gender?

What exactly is gender? How does it shape a person's experience of the world? Ideas about how men and women should behave and of what they are capable of changes depending on culture and environment. All people have unique gender identities. Some people identify as male or female. Some identify with neither category, known as **non-binary**. Some identify with both. The way that a person shows their identification to the world is called **gender expression**.

Even today, **stereotypes** and beliefs about gender create opportunities and set limits. We have made progress toward gender equality and opportunities for women, but much work remains to be done. The progress made also is threatened by recent crises such as the COVID-19 pandemic. It's up to us as members of a world community to continue pushing for positive change.

A common gender stereotype is that men are better leaders than women.

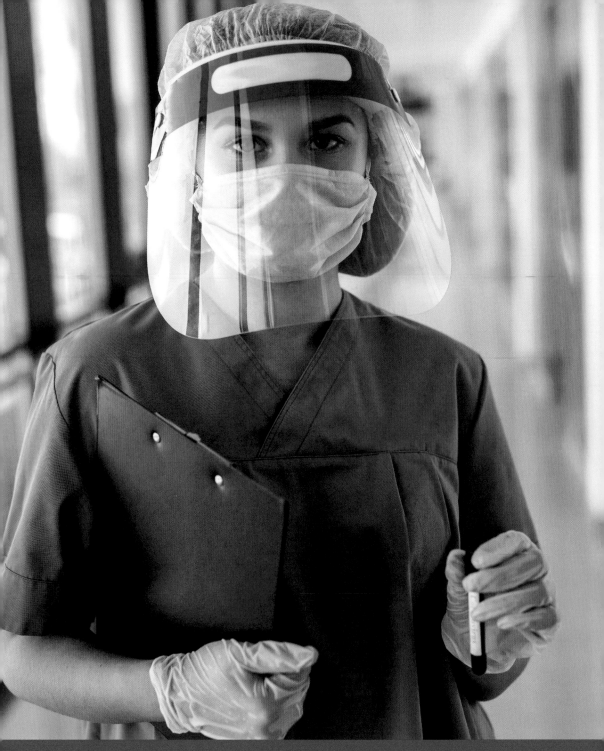

According to the UN statistics, women made up 70 percent of health care and social workers during the COVID-19 pandemic.

## Related Goals

Former UN Secretary-General Kofi Annan once said, "Gender equality is more than a goal in itself. It is a precondition for meeting the challenge of reducing poverty, promoting sustainable development, and building good governance." Annan makes an important point. Real progress in other SDGs like "No Poverty" and "Sustainable Cities and Communities" will also need action on gender equality.

Ready to help make SDG 5 a reality? Read on to learn about what's being done—and about what you can do—to build a gender-equal world.

> **STOP AND THINK:** *What does the word "equality" mean to you? How would you go about judging whether or not something was gender-equal?*

## COVID-19 and Closing the Global Gender Gap

The COVID-19 pandemic slowed gains in gender equality. Each year, the World Economic Forum releases a Global Gender Gap Report. In 2021, the report showed that closing the global gender gap will take 135.6 years—up from 99.5 years, as measured 1 year earlier.

# CHAPTER 2

# Why Do We Have Goals?

Chances are that you've set a goal. Maybe you wanted to run a mile in fewer than 8 minutes. Or you wanted to learn a new language or play a new instrument. To reach your goal, you probably came up with a plan. How would you start? What would you do each day to reach it? How would you measure your progress? When did you hope to complete it?

Without realizing it, you're probably using a "SMART" system for setting and reaching goals. "SMART" stands for Specific, Measurable, Achievable, Relevant, and Timed. This process isn't just used by individuals. Large organizations like the UN also use it to form a plan for meeting big global goals, including the SDGs.

**STOP AND THINK:** *What goals do you have? How could you use the SMART strategy to reach them?*

Barriers to education for girls around the world include distance to school, cultural norms, forced work or marriage, and violence.

Unpaid care work, like cooking, cleaning, and caring for children, keeps women from achieving full economic equality.

SDG 5 breaks down into several smaller targets:

- End all forms of discrimination against all women and girls everywhere.
- End violence and exploitation of women and girls.
- Eliminate harmful practices such as child marriage, early and forced marriage, and violence.
- Increase the value of unpaid care and promote shared domestic responsibilities.
- Ensure the full participation of women in leadership and decision-making.
- Ensure access to universal reproductive rights and health.
- Foster equal rights to economic resources, property ownership, and financial services for women.
- Promote empowerment of women through technology.
- Adopt, strengthen, and enforce legislation for gender equality.

Despite of the success of the U.S. Women's National Soccer Team, players still earn less than those on the men's team.

But the UN didn't stop at setting targets for SDG 5. The goal also includes measurable **indicators** that track progress on each point. People can act on these indicators to achieve results. Read more to learn about actions that you can take at home, at school, and in the larger world to help!

## Equal Pay for Equal Work

Gender pay gaps are a big issue worldwide. In the United States, women earn 81.8 cents to each dollar that a man doing the same job earns. The gap is worse for Latinx, Black, and **Indigenous** women, who earn 54 cents, 63 cents, and 57 cents to every male dollar.

In 2019, the World Cup-winning U.S. Women's National Soccer Team brought attention to this issue. Team members filed a lawsuit citing pay discrimination based on gender. It's not just an issue in the United States. The Jamaican Women's National Soccer Team has been working for equality since 2010. That year, sports officials cut program funding and players' pay.

# CHAPTER 3

# Do the Work! Contribute to the Goals at Home

How can you and your family work toward gender equality? Here are some ideas to get started:

- **Be Aware of Bias** — Be aware of the **biases** that you and others hold about gender, gender identity, and sexual orientation. Pay attention to what others say and to what is shown in the media. What stereotypes do you hear and see? When watching a TV show or movie or reading a book, try using the "Bechdel Test." This involves asking:
  - Does the movie, book, or TV show have at least two girls or women in it?
  - Do the girls or women talk to each other?
  - When they talk to each other, do they talk about something other than a boy or man?

You can use the Bechdel Test to ask similar questions to evaluate how LGBTQ+ people, religious groups, and people of color are represented on TV.

Boys and men can be allies in bringing about gender equality.

Whether we are aware of it or not, these media images influence our attitudes. Don't be afraid to challenge them! Talk about what you see with your family, neighbors, and friends. Write to filmmakers and authors to call out stereotypes. Through conversation, you can help push for non-biased representations.

- **Educate Yourself and Others** — Did you know that 47 percent of girls in Ethiopia who start first grade don't make it to fifth grade? Or that **transgender** people face a greater risk of violence and discrimination than **cisgender** people? Read about gender issues and challenges. Share what you've learned with others. And speak up against all forms of hate, discrimination, and violence.

- **Donate** — This year, consider skipping your birthday gifts. Instead, you can ask your family and friends to donate to organizations that support SDG 5. You could also host an event to support the UN's Global Fund for Women or a Kiva loan to a female entrepreneur. Your support can make a big difference in achieving gender equality and in making progress on related goals such poverty reduction and quality education.

# CHAPTER 4

# Do the Work! Contribute to the Goals at School

You and your classmates can help ensure that all girls have the right to go to school, thrive, and reach their full potential. Keep reading for some ideas on what you and your peers can do.

- **Learn** — Bring gender into the conversation in every subject area. Maybe it's questioning whose stories are studied in history class. Perhaps it's asking who gets represented as scientists and engineers in your textbooks. Don't be afraid to ask questions and push for change. You can also research organizations that work on gender equality in your community. You can invite members of these groups to talk to your class about gender-related issues.

Learn about STEM careers. Women only make up about 29 percent of the workforce in scientific research.

In 2021, Kamala Harris became the first female vice president of the United States. Globally, women make up 25 percent of national parliament and 36 percent of local elected officials.

- **Speak Up** — During one point in the 2020 vice presidential debate, Vice President Mike Pence interrupted candidate Kamala Harris. Harris responded, "Mr. Vice President, I'm speaking." If you find yourself in a similar situation, don't let yourself be silenced. Listen to others and insist on your right to speak and be heard.

- **Fundraise** — Like the high school drama club and California Girl Scout troop, you can fundraise on behalf of gender equality. It could be a rummage sale, a run/walk, or a "Battle of the Bands" event. Check the Malala Fund's website for further ideas and guidance on fundraising.

- **Clubs** — After-school or lunchtime clubs are a great way to investigate topics and issues that interest you. Want to know more about human rights? Consider starting an Amnesty International student group. Curious about coding? Research organizations like Girls Who Code, which help young women form coding clubs and close the gender gap in the tech industry.

STOP AND THINK: *What after-school activities are offered at your school? What groups would you join if they were offered? Ask a teacher about the best way to start a new club.*

# CHAPTER 5

# Do the Work! Contribute to the Goals in Your Community

January 21, 2017, marked the largest single-day protest in U.S. history. More than 5 million people took to the streets in cities all over the country. The occasion? A Women's March organized to support women's civil and reproductive rights.

Through organizing, marching, protesting, volunteering, and advocating, you can make a difference on SDG 5.

- **Raise Awareness** — Large public events like the 2017 Women's March draw attention to the continued need to address women's rights and equality issues. The Women's March inspired many women to speak out on gender-related issues.

The 2017 Women's March happened in cities throughout the United States and around the world.

- **Advocate** — Make sure that your lawmakers at the local, state, and national level know where you stand on the SDGs! Write letters, sign petitions, and call their offices to ask them to take action to create a more gender-equal world.

## Identity and Feminism

People experience gender differently based on factors such as race, religion, social class, sexual orientation, and ability. Think of your individual identity as a constellation formed from many stars. Each star might represent a different identity category. They combine to form the big picture that is YOU.

Events like the Women's March have led to conversations about who gets to make plans, speak, and be heard within the **feminist** movement. Many activists have urged White feminists to pay more attention to issues like racial bias and social class struggles. When you take action for the SDGs, remember that not everyone's experiences are like yours. Each person in the room has a story to tell. Listen to and learn from others.

# Extend Your Learning

## Background

Remember the Bechdel Test mentioned in Chapter 3? Think about the last book you read or movie you watched and use the Bechdel Test on it. Does it show women and girls as complex characters in their own right? Or are they are overshadowed by male figures in the story? The key questions to ask are:

- Does the movie, book, or TV show have at least two girls or women in it?
- Do the girls or women talk to each other?
- When they talk to each other, do they talk about something other than a boy or man?

## Act

Write a review of the book or movie to share with family, friends, and classmates. What "grade" do you give it on how it represents gender? Why? If you could rewrite the script or introduce new characters, what would you change? Ask other people in your life to share their thoughts on how the media can be more inclusive, less biased, and more representative.

# Further Research

## BOOKS

Cunningham, Kevin. *Can We Achieve Gender Equality?* Hallandale, FL: Mitchell Lane Publishers, 2020.

Felix, Rebecca. *#WomensMarch: Insisting on Equality.* Edina, MN: Abdo Publishing, 2020.

Mihaly, Christy. *Defining and Discussing Women's Rights.* Vero Beach, FL: Rourke Educational Media, 2020.

## WEBSITES

**Goal 5: Gender Equality and Empower All Women and Girls— United Nations Sustainable Development**
*https://www.un.org/sustainabledevelopment/gender-equality*
Check out the UN's Sustainable Development Goals website for more information on Goal 5.

**The Global Goals of Sustainable Development**
*margreetdeheer.com/eng/globalgoals.html*
Check out these free comics about the UNs Sustainable Development Goals.

# Glossary

**advocates** (ADD-vuh-kuhts) people who support a cause or claim

**biases** (BYE-uh-suhz) prejudices against a group

**cisgender** (siss-JEN-duhr) identifying with the sex (male or female) assigned at birth

**feminist** (FEH-muh-nihst) a person who recognizes and promotes the full equality of men and women

**gender** (JEN-duhr) socially created ideas about male and female behaviors and abilities

**gender expression** (JEN-duhr ik-SPREH-shuhn) how a person displays their gender, such as through clothing or behavior

**gender identities** (JEN-duhr eye-DEN-tuh-tees) a person's internal gender identity, which may or may not match the sex assigned at birth

**human trafficking** (HYOO-muhn TRAH-fuh-king) illegally transporting people without their consent for forced labor or exploitation

**indicators** (in-duh-KAY-tuhrs) measurements of progress

**Indigenous** (in-DIH-juh-nuhss) native to a place

**non-binary** (nahn-BYE-nuh-ree) a person who does not identify as either entirely male or female

**stereotypes** (STAIR-ee-uh-typz) common, fixed, or oversimplified ideas of a group of people

**sustainable** (suh-STAY-nuh-buhl) able to be maintained at a certain rate

**transgender** (trans-JEN-duhr) a person whose gender identity is different from that assigned at birth

**United Nations** (yuh-NYE-tuhd NAY-shuhns) the international organization that promotes peace and cooperation among nations

# INDEX

advocates/advocacy, 4, 27
Amnesty International, 25
Annan, Kofi, 11

Bechdel Test, 18, 19, 29
biases, 18, 21

care work, unpaid, 14, 15
child marriages, 4, 15
cisgender people, 21
"Climate Action" goal, 6
COVID-19, 8, 10, 11

"Decent Work and Economic
    Growth" goal, 6
decision-makers, 15
discrimination, 15, 17, 21

education, 4, 13, 22
elected officials, 24
empowerment of women, 15
equal pay, 16, 17
equality, 15
    economic, 14
    gender, 4, 11, 15, 20
Ethiopia, 21
exploitation, 4, 15

feminism, 28
fundraising, 25

gender, 21
    defined, 8
    equality, 4, 11, 15, 20
    pay gaps, 17
"Gender Equality and Women's
    Empowerment" goal, 5, 6
    contributing to goals at
        home, 18–21
    contributing to goals at
        school, 22–25
    contributing to goals in
        your community, 26–28
    overview, 7
    related goals, 11
    target goals, 15, 17

gender expression, 8
gender identity, 5, 8, 18, 28
girls
    and education, 4, 13, 22
    exploitation of, 4, 15
Girls Who Code, 4, 25
Global Fund for Women, UN, 21
Global Gender Gap Report, 11
goals, 12–17

Harris, Kamala, 24
hate, 21
human trafficking, 4

identity and feminism, 28
India, 4
indicators, measurable, 17
International Day of the Girl, 4

Kiva loans, 21

leadership, women, 15

Malala Fund, 25
Malawi, 4
marriage, 15
media, 18, 19, 21, 29
men and boys, 20
Mexico, 4

"No Poverty" goal, 6, 11

opportunities, equal, 4–5

"Partnership for the Goals," 6
pay, equal, 4, 17

"Quality Education" goal, 6

reproductive health and rights,
    15, 26
Russia, 6

SMART (Specific, Measurable,
    Achievable, Relevant, Timed)
    system, 12
STEM careers, 23
stereotypes, gender, 8, 9, 18, 21
"Sustainable Cities and
    Communities" goal, 11
Sustainable Development
    Goals (SDGs)
    overview, 4–11
    reason for, 6, 12–17
    related, 11
    what they are, 6

target goals, 15, 17
technology, 15, 25
transgender people, 21
TV shows, 18, 19

United Nations (UN), 5, 6, 12,
    17, 21
United States, 6
U.S. Women's National Soccer
    Team, 16, 17

violence, 4, 15, 21

women
    of color, 6
    and COVID-19, 10
    discrimination against, 15, 17
    and economic potential,
        6, 14, 15
    as elected officials, 24
    and employment, 6, 10, 23
    empowerment of, 15
    and equal pay, 16, 17
    exploitation of, 4, 15
    in leadership roles, 15
Women's March, 26–27, 28
women's rights, 6
World Economic Forum, 11